I0644350

BE YOUR BEST

INTEGRITY

Shannon Welbourn

AV2
www.av2books.com

Step 1
Go to **www.av2books.com**

Step 2
Enter this unique code

HAJUCJBZQ

Step 3
Explore your interactive eBook!

AV2 is optimized for use on any device

Your interactive eBook comes with...

Contents
Browse a live contents page to easily navigate through resources

Audio
Listen to sections of the book read aloud

Videos
Watch informative video clips

Weblinks
Gain additional information for research

Try This!
Complete activities and hands-on experiments

Key Words
Study vocabulary, and complete a matching word activity

Quizzes
Test your knowledge

Slideshows
View images and captions

... and much, much more!

View new titles and product videos at www.av2books.com

BE YOUR BEST

INTEGRITY

Contents

What Is Integrity?

"He is a person of integrity." When you hear a person described this way, do you know what it means?

Integrity is doing the right thing even when no one is watching. It means doing what you say you are going to do. It also means staying true to your beliefs. Everyone can develop integrity. To do so, you must first understand your beliefs of right and wrong. Your **morals** and **values** have an effect on your integrity. A value is something a person strongly believes. For example, being honest is a value. Morals are principles, or rules, that people follow in their lives. Your morals help you determine what you think is right and wrong. Integrity means you do what you know is right, even if things are difficult.

When you live your life with integrity, you are staying true to your morals and values. You keep your word and do what is right.

Why Is Integrity Important?

Understanding your own beliefs is important. When you understand your morals and values, you can build integrity.

Integrity develops from making good choices. You use your personal values to make choices. Consider your values and how they affect the choices you make. Personal values shape your behavior. They often form from your family's beliefs and values. They can also form from what your peers believe. Your values become **standards**.

For example, if cooperation is one of your values, you will strive to work well with others. When people use integrity to act and make decisions based on their beliefs, they are less likely to regret their choices.

These children are working together to help fix their friend's bike. This shows the value of helping others.

BIOGRAPHY

Joey Prusak

One way to show integrity is to help others by standing up for what is right. That is what teenager Joey Prusak did at the local ice cream shop where he worked.

One day, one of his regular customers came in for ice cream. This customer had a **visual impairment** and did not notice he dropped a $20 bill while leaving the store. Joey saw this happen, but before he could call out to the man, a woman picked up the money. Joey thought the woman was going to do the right thing and return it to the man. Instead she took the money and came to the front counter to order ice cream.

NAME: **Joey Prusak**
FROM: **Minneapolis, Minnesota**
ACCOMPLISHMENT: **Showed integrity by staying true to his beliefs and standing up for what is right**

Joey told the woman that he saw her take the money. He told her to return the money to the man or he would not serve her. She refused, and Joey asked her to leave the store. Joey then gave the man $20 of his own money to replace the money the woman took. Joey made a choice that shows he stayed true to his values. His story quickly spread online and serves as a good example of integrity.

Learn to Make Decisions

What other choices could Joey have made in this situation?

Joey Prusak was

19

years old when he helped the visually impaired customer.

Joey Prusak started working when he was

14

years old. He worked to save money for business school.

About

2.2 billion

people around the world have a form of visual impairment.

Integrity at Home

How you behave at home is important to your family. Showing integrity means that you respect your family members.

Your family members need to know they can trust you. You need to be **reliable**. People with integrity follow through on what is asked of them, even when no one is watching. Your parents give you the **responsibility** of feeding the family dog. You are about to leave for your baseball game when you notice his water dish is empty. You take the time to fill the dish before leaving. This shows integrity because you followed through on your **commitment** to feed your dog, even when you were on your way out the door and no one was around. And your dog will be thankful, too!

One way to show your integrity is by following through on what you say you are going to do. Finishing your chores before playing outside shows integrity.

Integrity at School

Acting with integrity involves doing the right thing and being responsible for your actions.

Being a dependable student means that you do the things that are expected of you. Coming to school prepared and ready to learn, and trying your best in class, shows your integrity.

Taking responsibility for your actions is a way that you can show integrity. When you do not finish homework, you may have to stay in at recess.

If you do not do your part in a group project, it will hurt others.

Having integrity means you should act or behave in a certain way. Your classmates and teacher need to know you will follow classroom rules, such as raising your hand to speak or treating peers with respect. Working in a group with other people means each of you agrees to do one part of a project. Each person needs to be responsible. Acting with integrity means that you follow your word and complete your part.

Learn to Make Decisions

What would you do if a friend asked to copy your answers on a test?

Integrity in Your Community

A community is a group of people who live, work, and play in a place. Your home, school, and neighborhood are part of your community.

Integrity is just as important in your community as it is at home and school. Many kids are part of teams and clubs in their communities. If you are on a soccer team, one of the rules is that you cannot touch the ball with your hands. If you do, the ball is given to the other team. Some players may try to hide that they touched the ball or argue with the referee that they did not touch it. The right thing to do is to admit you touched the ball, even if it gives the other team an advantage. It shows you have integrity when you are honest and do the right thing.

Following the rules shows integrity in all situations.

BIOGRAPHY

Matthew Kaplan

When Matthew Kaplan discovered that his younger brother, Josh, was being bullied, he decided to stand up for his values and make a difference.

Matthew founded the BE ONE Project, which stands for Be Open to New Experiences. His project encourages kids to act with integrity. Matthew felt that many kids who were bullying others did not realize how their actions were hurting these people. He believes that if all kids develop their morals and values and stay true to them, school communities can become more **inclusive** and positive for everyone. The BE ONE Project encourages kids to **reflect** on how their actions affect others. Kids also reflect on whether their actions follow their values, and take responsibility if they were involved in bullying.

NAME: **Matthew Kaplan**
FROM: **Phoenix, Arizona**
ACCOMPLISHMENT:
Founded the BE ONE Project to encourage integrity in students and stop bullying

Matthew visits schools and encourages kids to be role models for one another by being kind and accepting to everyone, even when no one is watching. He also encourages kids to hold each other **accountable** for their actions. This means that kids in a school community hold each other responsible for acting with integrity. Matthew hopes that with a little integrity, students can work together to make their school communities safe, accepting, and positive places for everyone.

Matthew Kaplan started the

BE ONE

project when he was

15

years old.

The BE ONE Project offers an anti-bullying program for kids in grades

5 to 8.

In 2017, about **20** percent of U.S. students between **12** and **18** years old experienced bullying.

"The solution lies in teaching students that we have the power to shape the culture in our schools."

—Matthew Kaplan

Overcoming Challenges

Acting with integrity is not always easy. It can be difficult. You can work on building integrity throughout your life.

Sometimes, we know what the right thing to do is, but we find it hard to do. It can be challenging to build integrity when we are tempted to play video games instead of following through on our commitment to finish our chores. Showing integrity can also be difficult when it seems easier to tell a lie than to be honest, such as telling your teacher that a dog ate your homework instead of admitting that you did not complete it. Even though it is not always easy, it is important to stay true to our values and practice integrity!

Remember the tips below to help make sure you act with integrity.

- Be honest, trustworthy, and reliable.
- Keep your values in mind.
- Always do what you believe is right.
- Follow your word. If you said you would do something, then do it.
- Think about how your actions will affect others.
- Always take responsibility for your actions.

Encouraging Integrity in Others

Promote integrity in your daily life by helping others stay true to their values, too.

Be a good example to your friends and others around you. Living your life with integrity shows others the type of person you are. People learn they can trust you. They know that you are reliable. Encourage others to act with honestly and fairness. Help them to understand how their decisions and actions build their character. Encourage others to act with integrity and stay true to their beliefs. Help them think about their morals and values.

Learn to Make Decisions

Write a list of your values. How can you show others your integrity by upholding what you believe?

When you treat others with kindness, honesty, and integrity, you receive much of the same in return.

Integrity in Action

In this book, you have learned why integrity is important and some of the ways people show it in their daily lives.

Read each of the examples and decide if the person's actions show integrity.
If you answer yes, explain your thinking.
If you answer no, describe how the person could change their actions to show integrity.

Sonya breaks her friend's toy by mistake. Her friend does not see her break it, so Sonya puts the toy back without telling her.

Dominic notices the new girl in his class has no one to play with during recess. He thinks about asking her to play tag with him and his friends. He decides to wait for someone else to play with her instead.

Malik has been on time for every swimming practice this summer. Today, he lost track of time and arrived 10 minutes late. He tells his coach he is sorry and will work hard to try to be on time next week.

Key Words

accountable: to take responsibility for actions
commitment: a promise to do something
inclusive: describing a group or space that is accepting or welcoming to all
morals: practices or beliefs held by a person, based on what is believed to be right and wrong
reflect: to think back on something
reliable: trustworthy
respect: giving things or people the attention they deserve
responsibility: the quality of being reliable or dependable
standards: morals, ethics, and values that determine thoughts and behaviors
values: things or qualities held to high esteem, or having importance to a person
visual impairment: having difficulty seeing

Index

Get the best of both worlds.

AV2 bridges the gap between print and digital.

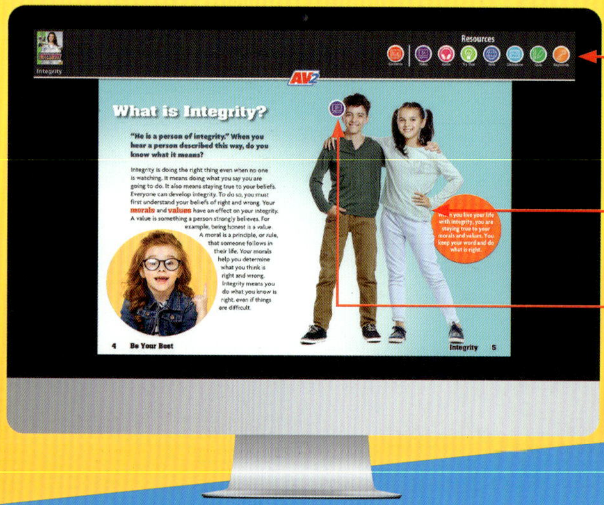

The expandable resources toolbar enables quick access to content including **videos**, **audio**, **activities**, **weblinks**, **slideshows**, **quizzes**, and **key words**.

Animated videos make static images come alive.

Resource icons on each page help readers to further **explore key concepts**.

Published by AV2
350 5th Avenue, 59th Floor
New York, NY 10118
Website: www.av2books.com

Copyright ©2021 AV2
All rights reserved. No part of this publication may be reproduced, stored in a retrieval system, or transmitted in any form or by any means, electronic, mechanical, photocopying, recording, or otherwise, without the prior written permission of the publisher.

Library of Congress Control Number: 2020937052

ISBN 978-1-7911-3162-3 (Hardcover)
ISBN 978-1-7911-3163-0 (Softcover)
ISBN 978-1-7911-3164-7 (Multi-user eBook)
ISBN 978-1-7911-3165-4 (Single-user eBook)

Printed in Guangzhou, China
1 2 3 4 5 6 7 8 9 0 24 23 22 21 20

042020
101119

Project Coordinator: Sara Cucini Designer: Jean Faye Marie Rodriguez

Every reasonable effort has been made to trace ownership and to obtain permission to reprint copyright material. The publishers would be pleased to have any errors or omissions brought to their attention so that they may be corrected in subsequent printings.

The publisher acknowledges Getty Images, iStock, and Shutterstock as its primary image suppliers for this title. Image p. 16 courtesy of Matthew Kaplan/The Be ONE Project.

First published by Crabtree Publishing Company in 2017.